WHY IS DADDY SAD ON SUNDAY?

A Coloring Book Depicting the Most Disappointing Moments in Cleveland Sports

By Scott O'Brien

Printed in Ohio, USA
by Bookmasters
Ashland, OH

This book is dedicated to my Mom & Dad,
my wife Jessie and daughter Mila,
the memory of Jody Hoop...

and especially all the long suffering Cleveland fans.

TABLE OF CONTENTS

THE DISAPPOINTMENTS

THE TRIUMPHS

SPECIAL THANKS

THE DISAPPOINTMENTS

THE CATCH

The first disappointing moment in our book may be the most iconic. The Indians enjoyed a decade of success leading up to the 1954 season, in which they captured a World Series victory in 1948. The 1954 season looked to eclipse even the prior achievements as the Indians set an American League record, winning 111 games. Matched up against the New York Giants, the Indians entered the series as the clear favorites. With the game tied and two men on in the top of the 8th inning, Indians first baseman Vic Wertz launched a long fly ball to centerfield. The hit would have been a homerun in most parks. However, this was the Polo Grounds which measured over 470 ft to the centerfield wall. With tremendous speed, Willie Mays caught up to the ball, made an amazing over-the-shoulder catch and whipped around getting a throw back to the infield. The runner on second base, caught off guard, may have been able to score the game-winning run if he did not have to return to the base to tag up. The Giants went on to win the game in extra innings, killing the Tribe's momentum, and they eventually swept the series. The Indians would not return to the World Series for another 41 years.

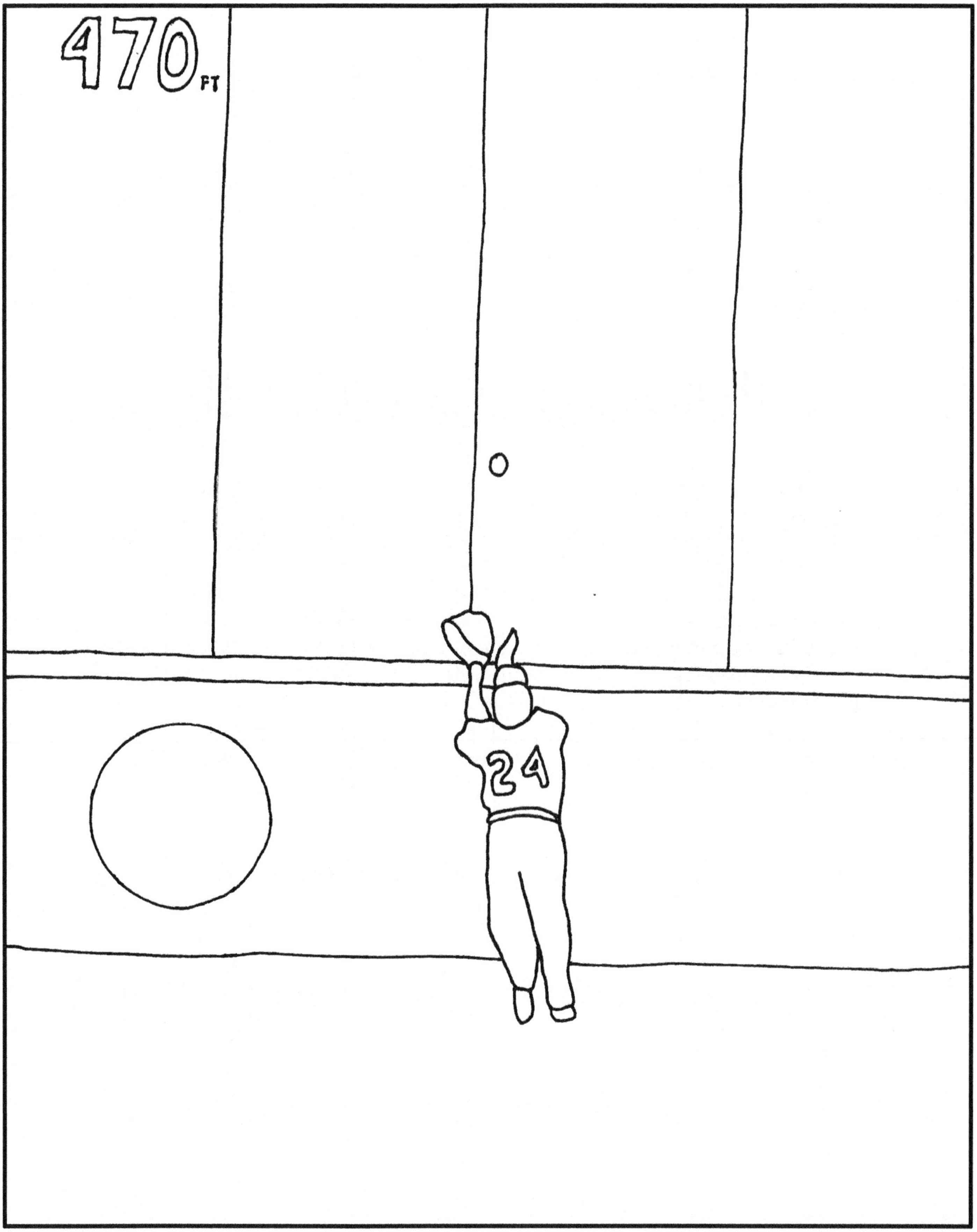
470 FT
24

THE CURSE OF ROCKY COLAVITO

The Tribe's success began to wane in the late 1950's, bringing to the scene a new GM, Frank "Trader" Lane, who was known for his wheeling and dealing. Notable Lane trades include sending home run gurus Roger Maris and Norm Cash away from Cleveland as they were entering their prime. But in 1960 he made the trade that he will always be remembered for when he traded fan favorite and home run champ Rocky Colavito to the Detroit Tigers for batting champ Harvey Kuenn. Indians fans were outraged by the trade. Colavito went on to make several All Star teams while with Detroit, whereas Kuenn was gone from Cleveland within one season. The trade became known locally as "The Curse of Rocky Colavito" and the Indians began their long slide into ineptitude.

THE 30 YEAR SLUMP

From 1960 to 1993, the Indians were the most irrelevant franchise in Major League Baseball. The best standing they achieved in their division during this period was third place... once... in 1968. Compounding the issues on the field was the aging and mammoth Cleveland Municipal Stadium, whose capacity was a staggering 74,438 people. Years of ineptitude had withered the fan base down to only the most loyal and the Tribe regularly played games to crowds of less than 10,000. To those watching from home, it looked as though the crowd was non-existent. Adding to the negative attention was the riot during the Tribe's 10 Cent Beer Night promotion, which painted the fans as crazed lunatics. In 1989, Hollywood made a film titled "Major League" which depicted a fictionalized version of the Cleveland Indians. In the film, the hapless Tribe somehow stumbled their way to winning the pennant despite the organization's best efforts to thwart them. Fans craved a contender and were about to get one...

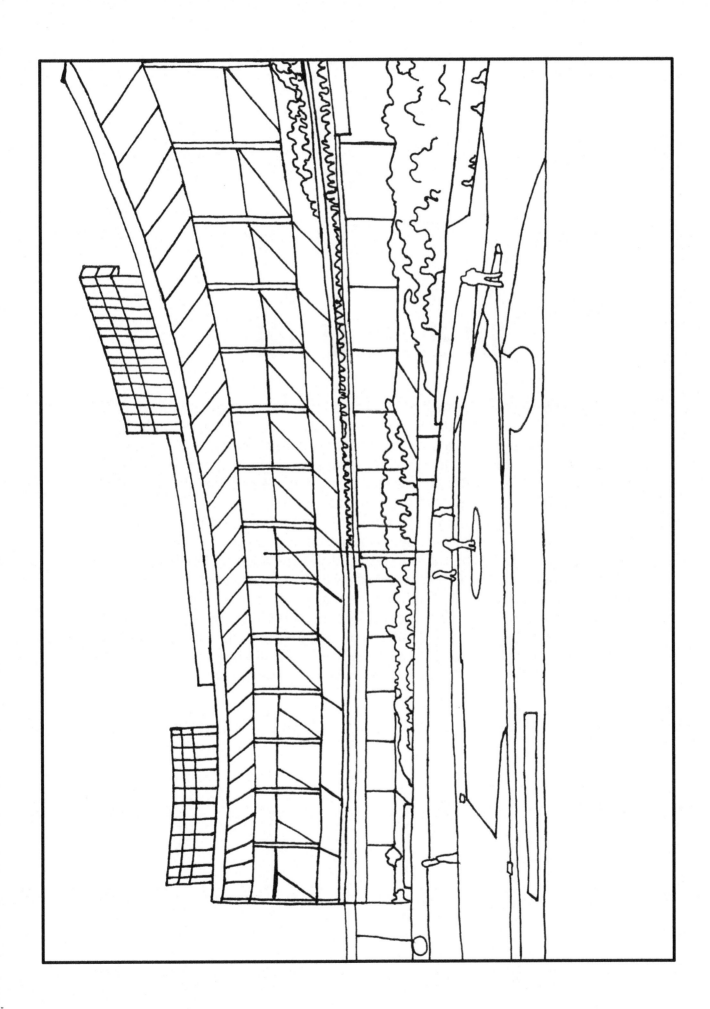

JIM BROWN RETIRES

By 1965, the Cleveland Browns had appeared in 11 NFL championship games in the previous 15 years and won four of them. They were the most dominating franchise of that time and also a strong contender for the upcoming season behind their star running back, Jim Brown. Arguably the best running back to ever play the game, Jim Brown was in his prime in 1965 and looking to make his 10th Pro Bowl appearance in the 1966 season. His popularity on the field allowed him to branch out and pursue a film career in the offseason. This quickly became a tense subject between Brown and Cleveland's new owner, Art Modell (kids remember that name), and the situation boiled over when Brown wished to remain on the set of a film for a few weeks instead of beginning training camp. Modell fined the star for every day of camp that he missed. The fines, as well as other factors, caused Jim Brown to decide to retire after the 1965 season and Modell did little to intervene. Another beloved Cleveland athlete was gone and the Browns have not won an NFL championship game or played in a Super Bowl since.

RED RIGHT 88

The 1981 AFC divisional playoff game at Cleveland Stadium was one of the coldest ever. It was a low scoring game in which there were several missed field goals and points were at a premium. Late in the 4th quarter, the Browns, who were known as the "Kardiac Kids" for their heart-stopping late-game comebacks that season, looked poised to pull off another one. Trailing 14-12 with less than one minute left in the game, the Browns had the ball on the Raiders' 13 yard line. Normally, a field goal of this distance is practically a sure-thing that would have won the game, however with the game conditions and the earlier misses on his mind, Browns coach Sam Rutigliano opted for an end zone pass play on 3rd down. The play, called Red Right 88, was intended for sure-handed Browns tight end Ozzie Newsome. Instead, the pass was intercepted by Oakland and iced the game, knocking the Browns out of the playoffs. Browns fans were shocked and dismayed at the turn of events. Oakland went on to win the Super Bowl that year, while the Browns would have to wait until 1985 for another shot at the championship.

TED STEPIEN RULE

The owner of the Cleveland Cavaliers from 1980 to 1983 was an interesting man named Ted Stepien. Not content to just write checks and leave the team management to the experts, Stepien appointed himself as the team GM and immediately began making decisions which raised eyebrows. He wrote huge checks to aging veterans, allegedly threatened to move the team to Toronto and traded away draft picks like they were going out of style. *The New York Times* described the Cavaliers during the Stepien years as "the worst club and most poorly run franchise in professional basketball." This was just the tip of the iceberg however, as Stepien's mismanagement not only crippled the Cavaliers for years to come, but also resulted in an NBA rule designed to prevent such a colossal failure from ever occurring again. Known as the "Ted Stepien Rule," the NBA now prohibits teams from trading first-round draft picks in successive seasons. After the team was sold to the Gund family in 1983, the Cavs were awarded extra draft picks to compensate for the damage done during Ted Stepien's reign.

THE DRIVE

Behind young quarterback, Bernie Kosar, and the best defense in the league, the Browns surged to the best record in the AFC in the 1986 season. They clinched home-field advantage throughout the playoffs and looked to be poised to play in their first Super Bowl. An amazing overtime, come-from-behind victory against the Jets in the divisional round set up the AFC championship game at Cleveland Stadium versus the Denver Broncos. As with almost every playoff game at Municipal Stadium, the conditions were cold and windy and not ideal for a high-scoring offensive game. So, with 5:11 left in the game, a 7 point lead, the league's best defense and the Broncos pinned on their own 2 yard line, Cleveland fans could taste a Super Bowl berth. That's when the unthinkable happened. Bronco's quarterback, John Elway, led Denver on a 98 yard drive that culminated in a game-tying touchdown with 39 seconds left in the game, sending it to overtime. Browns fans were devastated when the Broncos kicked a field goal to win the game in overtime. The kick appeared to hook wide left above the upright, but was nonetheless called fair by the officials. The Denver Broncos had just become Cleveland's biggest nemesis of the 1980's and the pain would not stop soon.

THE FUMBLE

In 1987, the Browns duplicated the success of the previous year and cruised to the AFC championship game against their archrival, the Denver Broncos. Unlike the previous meeting, the Browns were behind for most of the game and found themselves down 7 points with 6 minutes remaining. As Kosar drove the team down the field, it appeared that Denver was about to be on the losing end of the comeback this time around. With the ball on Denver's 8 yard line and just over a minute remaining, Kosar handed the ball off to stellar running back, Earnest Byner. It looked like Byner had a clear path to a touchdown, but at the last second he was stripped of the ball by a Denver defender. The Broncos recovered the fumble and held on for the win, heading to their second Super Bowl in two years. The Browns, once again, so close to the big game they could taste it, were dealt a crushing blow by Elway and the Broncos.

THE SHOT

The Cavaliers of the late 1980's and early 90's were some of the more talented teams in the franchise's history. Behind head coaches Lenny Wilkens and Mike Fratello, they appeared in the playoffs 8 of 9 seasons from 1988 to 1996. There were high expectations for them when they met the young Chicago Bulls in the first round of the playoffs in 1989. The Bulls had talent in Michael Jordan, but were certainly the underdog after the Cavs swept all four games of the season series. At home in Cleveland, in the last game of the best of five series, the Cavs traded shots with the Bulls down the stretch and clung to a one point lead after a Craig Ehlo layup with 3 seconds left to play. The Bulls called a timeout and then inbounded to Jordan, who made room between himself and Ehlo, then hit a foul line jumper as time expired to win the game and clinch the series for the Bulls. Cavs fans could only sit and stare as Jordan leaped in triumph. Chicago was just getting ready to begin their first dynasty, while Cleveland would experience several more disappointing early playoff exits in the years to come, including another that ended with a similar shot from Michael Jordan.

THE 1995 WORLD SERIES

After 35 years of futility, the 1995 Indians dominated the regular season, finishing the strike-shortened year with a 100-44 record. They also cruised through the AL playoffs behind a young core of solid hitters and a very strong pitching staff, finding themselves in the World Series for the first time since 1954. The Indians had reason to be confident entering the series, as they were arguably the most balanced team in Major League Baseball. However, the Braves had one of the most talented pitching staffs of the time, which the Indians were unable to overcome. The duo of aces Tom Glavine and Greg Maddux won three of the four games they started and the Indians ended up losing the series in six games. Adding to the disappointment for Cleveland fans was the fact that five of the games were decided by one just run. A few breaks for the Tribe could easily have sent the series in the opposite direction.

THE MOVE

The early 1990's found the Browns in a transition phase after their mostly successful run in the 80's. New head coach, Bill Belichick, cut fan favorite quarterback, Bernie Kosar, for what he referred to as "diminishing skills" and the franchise found itself mired in losing seasons. The franchise started to turn around and head in the right direction in 1994 with a short playoff run. The start of the 1995 season looked very promising after the strong performance of the previous year.

At the same time, Browns owner Art Modell, began voicing his displeasure with the financial state of his team, which he blamed on an old stadium and declining revenues. Despite having the most loyal fan base in professional sports, Modell claimed he was unable to make money operating the Cleveland Browns in Municipal Stadium. Modell was also allegedly withdrawing more and more from negotiations with the city to renovate the stadium. Art had become obsessed with getting a new stadium like the ones that were being built or planned for NFL teams in other cities.

On November 6, 1995 Art Modell, a man who had previously denounced the moves of other teams, announced that he had finalized plans to move the beloved Browns to Baltimore. Fans were shocked and dismayed. The city filed an injunction, advertisers withdrew their support, there were fan rallies led by TV star and Cleveland native Drew Carey and even congressional hearings, but the move proceeded and Cleveland lost their football team. The one bright spot of this dark time was that the city was able to save the "Browns" name, colors and history for a future NFL team. They would eventually receive that team in 1999 when Modell's alleged co-conspirator, Al Lerner, "helped" bring football back to Cleveland by taking ownership of the new Browns. The new Baltimore team, the Ravens, went on to win the Super Bowl in 2000 and 2012 while the Browns have been one of the most losing teams in the NFL since their return.

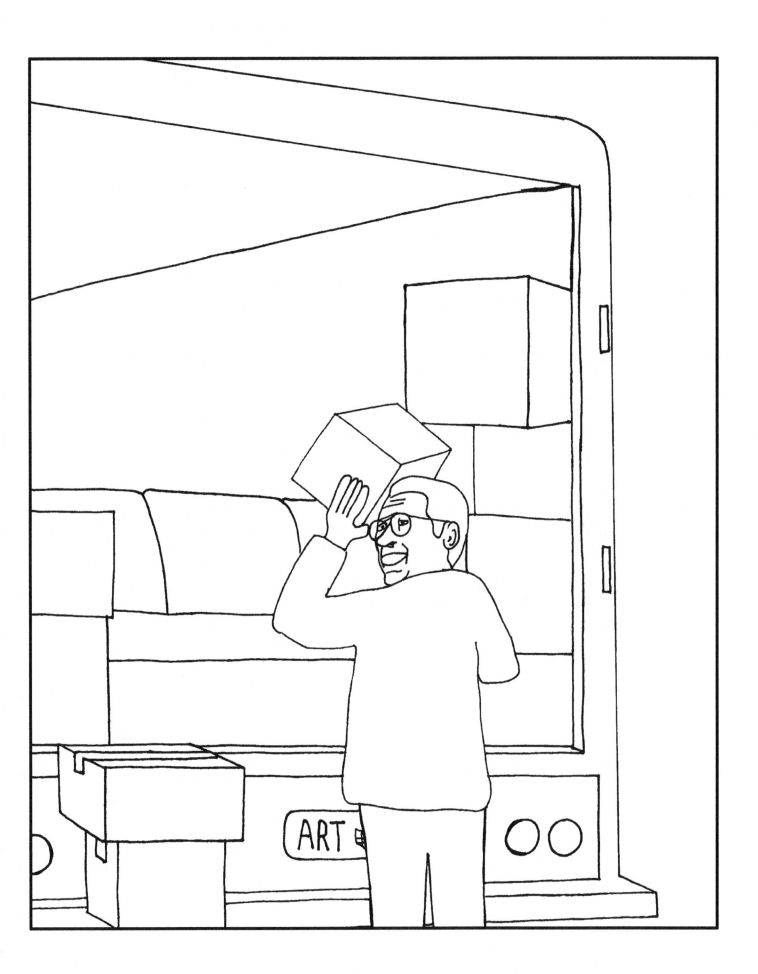

THE 1997 WORLD SERIES

Two years after their disappointing loss to the Braves, the Indians again earned their way to the World Series in 1997. Cleveland finished the regular season strong behind the solid hitting of stars Manny Ramirez, Jim Thome and David Justice. This time around, the Tribe came into the series as the strong favorite over the National League champion, the Florida Marlins. The teams traded wins over the first six games of the series in what were mostly lopsided victories. This World Series also featured a game in Cleveland that still holds the record for the coldest game in the series history. However, Game 7 took place in balmy Florida and saw the Indians carry a 1 run lead into the bottom of the ninth inning. The Indians were confident as they sent their shut-down closer, Jose Mesa, to the mound to wrap up the game and the series. Unfortunately for Cleveland fans, Mesa blew the save by giving up a run in the ninth and sending the game to extra innings. Finally, Edgar Renteria's single off Nagy's glove in the bottom of 11th sealed the heartbreak for Indians fans everywhere. The Indians became the first team in league history to lose Game 7 of the World Series after carrying a lead into the ninth inning.

DWAYNE RUDD HELMET TOSS

There weren't many bright spots for the Browns after returning to the league in 1999, but the 2002 season and its playoff berth could be considered the high water mark. One of the more memorable moments from this season occurred in the home opener. The Browns 2.0 had not experienced much success in home openers over the years, but stumbled their way to a 39-37 lead over the Kansas City Chiefs with 10 seconds left in the game. As KC quarterback, Trent Green, dropped back to pass, the Browns defense smothered him in what appeared to be a game clinching sack. Browns linebacker, Dwayne Rudd, took off his helmet and threw it in the air in celebration of his game ending play. However, he did not see that just before going down, Green had lateraled the ball to his offensive lineman who ran it to the Browns 26 yard line as time expired. Normally, this would have been the end of the game, but because Rudd had thrown his helmet, the Browns were given an "unsportsmanlike conduct" penalty. Under NFL rules, a game can not end with a defensive penalty, so the Chiefs were allowed one more play from the Browns 13 yard line. They kicked an easy field goal to win the game by one point. While this loss was a tough pill to swallow for Browns fans, it would not compare to the pain which followed their playoff game later that year.

STEELERS COMEBACK

After an embarrassing loss in the home opener, the Browns managed to right the ship in time to finish the 2002 season with a 9-7 record, which clinched them a spot in the playoffs after prevailing in several tiebreakers. Unfortunately, the Browns would have to head to Pittsburgh to face their rival to whom they lost both games in the regular season. Despite entering the game as a major underdog, the Browns managed to lead the entire game and at one point, were up by 17 points. However, with three minutes remaining, the Browns were clinging to a 33-28 lead. Unable to run down the clock after a series of miscues; they were forced to punt. That is when Pittsburgh's backup quarterback, Tommy Maddux, lead them on a 58 yard drive which was capped with a three yard touchdown run by Fuamatu-Ma'afala. Cleveland was unable to respond in the little remaining time and exited the playoffs. Browns fans were stunned to see their team torched for over 300 yards by a journeyman backup QB. The game also marked Pittsburgh's largest postseason comeback in franchise history. The Browns have not seen the postseason since.

RICKY DAVIS TRIPLE DOUBLE

In 2003, the Cavs found themselves at the bottom of a downward trajectory which had begun nearly a decade before. There were very few bright spots and the team seemed to be disinterested in winning. Many journalists speculated that the Cavs were hoping to obtain more chances at the first pick in the upcoming NBA draft lottery and the rights to a certain future MVP who resided a few miles away. Somehow, on March 3rd, the Cavs managed to run away to a 120-95 lead over the visiting Utah Jazz late in the 4th quarter. With the game pretty much decided, Cavs forward, Ricky Davis, set his sights on a personal goal: his first career triple-double. With only a few seconds left on the clock, and one rebound shy of his goal, Davis bounced the ball off his own rim and grabbed the basketball. The fans were stunned, and Davis received a hard foul from a Utah player for his unsportsmanlike move. The referees had never seen someone shoot at their own basket before, and not knowing how to react, allowed play to resume. The rebound was played constantly by the sports media and Davis became known to Cleveland fans as "Wrong Rim Ricky."
He never got credit for that triple-double.

2007 ALCS

After missing the postseason the previous five years, a young and talented Indians squad made their way to the American League Championship series in 2007. Behind two 19 game-winning starting pitchers, CC Sabathia and Fausto Carmona, Cleveland achieved beyond fans expectations that year and looked to be peaking at the right time to make a deep postseason run. The Indians took the division series over the New York Yankees in four games. One notable event that took place in this series was the famous "bug game." The Tribe was down by one run late in the game, when the Yankees brought in their heralded set-up pitcher Joba Chamberlain. As he began pitching in the 8th inning, a swarm of Lake Erie midges descended on the field distracting the pitcher. Play was stopped and when Chamberlain resumed, he ended up giving up the tying run and sending the game to extra innings, where the Indians prevailed. Unfortunately for Cleveland, the good luck did not continue into the next series.

The ALCS matched the Indians up with the heavy favorites, the Boston Red Sox. Game 1 looked to be a preview of how the series was to play out after the Red Sox handily defeated the Indians and Cy Young award winner Sabathia, 10-3. However, the Indians responded by taking the next 3 games and looked poised to upset Boston, as the Red Sox would need to defeat both of Cleveland's aces in order continue the series. The unthinkable happened when Boston took the last three games of the series in convincing fashion. Cleveland fans were dismayed to see the fairytale season end one game shy of the World Series, which Boston eventually went on to win. The Indians would not see the postseason again until their 2013 one game wildcard loss to the Rays.

2009 EASTERN CONFERENCE FINALS

The 2008-09 Cavaliers appeared to be unstoppable. Behind NBA MVP, Lebron James, they went 66-16 in the regular season and swept the first two rounds of the playoffs, winning every game by at least 10 points. The team had clinched home court advantage throughout the playoffs and saw their next opponent, the unproven Orlando Magic, as a minor roadblock to their second NBA finals in three years. Most analysts believed that the Cavs were destined for the Finals and their best chance in franchise history at winning a championship. The team was caught off guard and stunned when the Magic came back from a large deficit to take Game 1 of the Eastern Conference Finals with a late three point dagger of a shot. The Cavs barely survived Game 2 on a miraculous last second three-pointer by Lebron James. Cleveland was not so lucky the rest of the series, dropping three of the last four games, and heading home after a season of so much promise. Cavs fans began a year of anxiety, as James was heading into the last season of his contract and they knew the 2009-10 season would be all-or-nothing if they wanted to keep their hometown star.

THE COLLAPSE

"A ring for the king!" is what future hall-of-fame center, Shaquille O'Neal, promised when the Cavs signed him before the start of the 2009-10 season. Everyone knew that the if team wanted to ensure that "The King," aka Lebron James, would stay in Cleveland after this year, they would need nothing less. The Cavs organization also made it clear that they would stop at nothing to put the team in the best position to win it all. For the second year in a row, Cleveland finished with the best record in the NBA and looked like a true championship contender. The Cavs easily handled the Chicago Bulls in the first round of the playoffs and prepared to face their nemesis, the Boston Celtics, in the second round. Although Cleveland had experienced a lot of trouble with the Celtics in the past, most fans believed that the Boston stars were aging and that the Cavs now had the experience to take the upper hand in the rivalry. However, fans were also anxious about a mysterious elbow injury that Lebron had apparently suffered which caused him to attempt a left-handed free throw in the previous series. No structural damage could be seen in X-rays and MRIs but that did not stop the media from round-the-clock speculation.

The first three games of the series with Boston saw wild, lopsided wins for both teams, with the Cavs taking a 2-1 lead. However, in the last two games James appeared distant and shot just 11-35. Rumors started circling of late-night parties and supposed betrayals by Cavalier players, which was causing the lack of focus. The most confusing part of the series came at the end of Game 6 with the Cavs facing elimination. With over a minute and a half remaining, and down only seven points, the Cavs appeared to be giving up on the game (and the season) and did not foul to preserve the clock despite Coach Mike Brown's desperate pleas to have the team do so. The last minute of the game also saw several Cavs turnovers and even a rare three point attempt from center, Anderson Varejao, who rarely was advised to attempt even short-range shots. As time expired, so did the Cavs' championship hopes. As Lebron walked down the tunnel, he tore off his jersey and Cavs fans felt their stomachs drop as they wondered if it was for the last time.

THE DECISION

From the moment the Cavs were dismissed from the 2010 NBA playoffs, the focus of the national sports media turned to the topic of where Lebron James would end up after free agency. Having underachieved the previous three seasons, the Cavs decided to part ways with coach Mike Brown. Analysts speculated that the move was made in the hopes of appeasing James. However, Lebron remained silent on his intentions as he began meeting with courting teams in his Cleveland office.

Shortly after free agency began, Toronto forward Chris Bosh decided to sign with the Miami Heat to join their star, Dwyane Wade. Rumors began to circulate that Lebron had already decided to join them in Miami. Insiders claimed that the three, who played together on Team USA in the 2008 Olympics, had previously discussed joining forces once the contracts with their current teams were up. Cleveland fans, as well as the Cavs organization, seemed to ignore this possibility and believed that James was far too rooted in Northeast Ohio to part ways so easily.

As the free agency season progressed, the Cavs hired a new head coach, Byron Scott, who insiders believed was picked in order to fit with LeBron's desire to be coached by a former NBA player. However, the Cleveland front office began to get nervous as LeBron was reportedly rebuffing Scott's phone calls and was stonewalling the organization's other attempts to contact him.

ESPN soon started promoting a television special titled "The Decision," set to air on July 8th, during which Lebron would announce where he would be signing. Hours before the scheduled announcement, rumors began to spread that Lebron was indeed headed to the Miami Heat. However, there had been so many rumors over the previous weeks that it was hard to know which one was true. In a packed Connecticut gymnasium, in front of the backdrop of young Boys & Girls Club members, Lebron confirmed the rumors that he was indeed "taking his talents to South Beach." The reaction in Cleveland was immediate. Fans were shocked and devastated and renounced the hometown star. Cavaliers owner, Dan Gilbert, who seemed as in the dark as anyone else regarding the decision, wrote a passionate letter to the fans in his preferred font of *Comic Sans*, which guaranteed that the Cavs would "win a championship before the self-titled former 'King' wins one." The Cavs have not seen the playoffs since and James has won two titles in three seasons with the Miami Heat.

THE QB BUNCH

Tim Couch, Ty Detmer, Doug Pederson, Spergon Wynn, Kelly Holcomb, Jeff Garcia, Luke McCown, Trent Dilfer, Charlie Frye, Derek Anderson, Brady Quinn, Ken Dorsey, Bruce Gradkowski, Colt McCoy, Jake Delhomme, Seneca Wallace, Brandon Weedon, Thad Lewis, Jason Campbell, and Brian Hoyer. These are the starting quarterbacks since 1999 for your Cleveland Browns! For those playing along at home, that list consists of 20 starting QBs in 15 years. Not exactly a model of consistency. And as we approach the 2014 season, it looks like the list will be growing...

*Clockwise from upper left on the opposite page: Tim Couch, Charlie Frye, Derek Anderson, Trent Dilfer, Brandon Weeden, Colt McCoy, Brady Quinn, Jeff Garcia

THE THREE STOOGES

When new owner, Jimmy Haslem, took over the Browns in October of 2012, he promised consistency and accountability for the team. He also promised to give the current coach and front office an opportunity to prove their value. The next day he hired a new CEO, Joe Banner, to oversee the current front office and staff.

As the 2012 season progressed, and the team continued to flounder, it seemed as though coach Pat Shurmer and his staff were dead men walking. On New Year's Eve, with the Browns months out of the playoff chase and the regular season over, the current front office and coaching staff was let go. Haslem promised fans that he would do his due diligence and hire a new front office and coach that would right the ship, but he also asked the fans to bear with him as the team embarked on a another "rebuilding" year. Fans had heard this pitch before.

The organization hired a new General Manger, Mike Lombardi, and a new head coach, Rob Chudzinski. Fans wanted Chudzinski, a locally raised, self-proclaimed Browns fan, to succeed. But as the 2013 season progressed, it became apparent that this team was no different than the teams before it and another season was lost. Most analysts and fans presumed that the staff would be given at least another year to show improvement as, after all, it was Haslem who had preached the merits of consistency and it was his front office who chose Chudzinski. However, at the end of the season, Cleveland fans saw yet another coach fired. Browns fans were frustrated since it appeared that there was no progress made at all in the two years since Haslem had taken over. In a press conference discussing the recent firing and new direction of the team, a local reporter, referring to the trio of Haslem, Banner and Lombardi, asked if they could "assure the fans that you don't have the three stooges running this organization." Haslem took the question in stride, but a new nickname for the front office was born. A few months later, Banner and Lombardi were also let go. The Browns had now burned through 20 starting quarterbacks, 7 head coaches, and 6 general mangers in 15 seasons... but who's counting?

THE TRIUMPHS

1950 NFL CHAMPIONSHIP

Before the merger of the two professional football leagues into the NFL, the Browns dominated the AAFC, winning all four championships in the late 1940's. Victories were so lopsided, that the AAFC sent top Cleveland Browns players to other teams. Despite this success, the NFL claimed that the Browns were untested and were no match for their teams. After the merger of the two leagues at the end of 1949, the Browns had the opportunity to prove their dominance in a title game versus the previous NFL league team, the Los Angeles Rams. The game was hosted in Cleveland at Municipal Stadium in front of a crowd of over 29,000 people on a cold, Christmas Eve day. The Browns fell behind 28-20 in the 4th quarter, but managed a comeback behind Hall of Fame quarterback, Otto Graham, icing the game with a Lou "The Toe" Groza field goal with 0:28 seconds left. The Browns went on to play in 11 NFL championships in the 1950's and 60's, winning four of them.

THE MIRACLE OF RICHFIELD

The Cleveland Cavaliers were added to the NBA as an expansion franchise in 1970. As with most expansion teams, the early years consisted of several losing seasons while the team built up to success. Surprisingly, the 1975-76 season saw a young Cavs team win the Central division and earn a trip to their first playoffs. Matched up against the Washington Bullets in the semifinal series, the Cavaliers were the clear underdogs. However due to their superior record, Cleveland had home-court advantage at the newly built Richfield Coliseum. The series was close, with three of the four Cleveland wins coming down to last second shots, the last of which occurred in Game 7 when Dick Snyder put up a huge shot over Phil Chenier to clinch the series. Locally, the series became known as "The Miracle of Richfield."

1995 PENNANT VICTORY

From 1960 to 1993, the Indians were one of the worst teams in baseball and fans began to wonder if they would ever see a pennant win again. The team was in contention in 1994, only to have the rest of the season (and postseason) cancelled by a players' strike. With the strike resolved shortly into the 1995 season, the Indians came out of the gate strong and ended up winning 100 of their 144 games that year and making the postseason for the first time since 1954. The Tribe cruised through the playoffs, defeating the Red Sox in three games and the Mariners in six to clinch their first pennant in over forty years!

DEVOTED BROWNS FANS
MICHAEL MURPHY & FAMILY!

"Despite the title of this book, some of my best memories growing up in Cleveland stem from going to Browns games with my father. The memories are still vivid. December, bundled up in the warmest clothes I owned, late in the 4th quarter, daylight almost gone, Browns on defense protecting a slim lead, opposing team pinned in the Dawg Pound end of the stadium, fans making so much noise that the opposing QB calls a timeout, and then, like magic, the snow starts falling and the volume from the Browns faithful gets louder. A curious thing happens in Cleveland with a playoff-bound Browns team: no one even knows it's winter until sometime in January. The energy keeps the whole city warm. We had season tickets from 1987 through 1995 and there are too many great memories to recount here but some highlights include: Ozzie Newsome's streak of receptions in 150 consecutive games, Ron Wolfley hustling down the field to cover a kickoff or slipping though the line to catch a short TD pass from Kosar or Testaverde, journeyman QB Don Strock leading the Browns to a victory over the Oilers at snowy Municipal Stadium. Beyond these, we had a lot of favorite players that I emulated in backyard games with friends including Carl "Big Daddy" Hairston, Clay Matthews, Hanford Dixon, Frank Minnifield, Brian Brennan, Webster Slaughter, Kevin Mack, Reggie Langhorne, Gerald "The Ice Cube" McNeil, and DD Hoggard.
Thanks dad!"

-Michael Murphy

*Shown from left to right on the opposite page: Patrick Murphy, Michael Murphy and Helena Murphy

THANK YOU!

Without support from the following people, this book would not have been possible:

The Murphy Family
3 Apple Generations: Stan/Seth/Shayne
Aaron Gilak
Aaron M. Hoopes
Aaron Paulley
Abrams Family
Adam
Adam Barhorst
Adam Benedict
Adam Brown
Adam Divelbiss
Adam Erhard
Adam Manella
Adam Maxson
Adam Oliveri
Adam Schmidt
Addison Claire James
Aine Donovan
Alan & Patti Burjoski
Alan Cool
Alec Gilchrist
Alei Ruhlman
Alex Calfee
Alex Halovanic
Alex Shively, Max Minnillo,
    Sean Suttle, Jeff Stevens
Alexander Ralston
Alfred Bertleff
Ally Millar
Alphonso Samano
Alyson Apel
Amanda Detki
Amanda Hammill
Amanda Kratzer
Amy "Tell me when it's over" Sheldon
Amy Asbury Walton - still a fan!
Amy Engdahl
Amy Keating & Dave Lucas

Andre Nintcheff
Andrea Hershberger
Andrea Lukuch
Andrew Cornell
Andrew Harey
Andrew J. Breitenbach
Andrew Stephen
Andrew Swab
Andrew Tyler
Andrew Zucker AKA "Mr. Moose"
Andy Dobbing
Angela Simone
Angie Gudaitis
Ann K. Hanrahan
Anonymous
Anthony Hunter
Anthony Huss
Anthony J Garafolo
Anthony Miranda and John Rieker
April Ledebur
Art Modell
Artie Routh
Artin Bastani
Austin J. Schmidt
Austin Ratner
B Rey
Baby Rychel
Ben "Sips" White
Ben Fuller
Benjamin Fahey
Benjamin Grafchik
Bert White
Beth & Tim Dentler
BH
Big D, E & Nick Smith
Bill Bowers
Bill Burmeister
Bill Cook - Lima, Ohio

Bill Patterson - Disappointed Since 1963!
Bill Reel Sr.
Bill Rittenhouse
Bill Small
Bob "Papa D" Delnoce
Bob & Danielle Kucharski
bob & pat lang
Bob Boester
Bob Keeney, Suffering Since 1980
Bob Michaels
Bobby Essler
Brad "Kick-Ass Offense" Childress
Brad Tingquist
Branden and Tracey Drake
Brandon Blosser
Brandon English from Shaker Heights
Brandon Jablonski
Brandon Thomas
Bree, Anth, Jess, Rox & Quinn Slota
Brendan & Jenny Meara
Brent Pemberton
Bret Kiraly
Bri Laukitis and Joe Benden
Brian Alleman
Brian D. Evancic
Brian Delany
Brian Emch
Brian Goddard
Brian I Magnani
Brian Malinowski (love to Dad)
Brian Novatny
Brian P. Downing, American Folk Legend
Brian Price
Brian Schiller
Brian Siegel
Brian T. Cherry
Brian Wood
Brie McCartney
Brigid Gurry
Bruce Bailey
Bruce Danford
Bruckners, Shoemakers, &
    Schneringers
Bryan Geraghty for Dillon Bilek

Bryan, Emily, and Baby G
Bryce & Brayden Seabold
Calvin "Dick" Lint
Canton, Ohio
Carol Sweet
Carter "Papa" Lewis and family
Caryn Evans
Catherine F
Celeste Patti
Chad Middleton
charles adkinson
Charles Ebner
Charles 'Grandpa' Walker
Charles Reynolds
Charley Jacobs
Charlie Mertz
Charlie Rich
Chris "Schotz" Schatschneider
Chris Durr
Chris Keck
Chris Lawton
Chris Sirc
Chris Stacy
Chris Szabo
Christopher and Dawn Noll
Christopher M. Stroup
Christopher Noice
Christopher Ross
Christopher Yanni, Rachel Kelly
Christy Frank
Chuck Edgar
Chuck Taylor
City By The Lake Fan
Claudia Sacks Schumer & John Sacks
Cleveland sports love forever... Jeff Rose
Clint Kakstys
Clyde Witt
Colin D. Campbell
Colin McNamara
Conor Higgins
Conrad
Corey LaRue
Crafty Mart
Craig and Connor Shore

Craig Shore
Craig Stair
Curt Fell
Curt Mohney
D. Eduardo Grunyon
Dale Stincic
Dallas Area Browns Backers
Dan & James Begallie
Dan and Joanne Young - Go Browns
Dan Buckler
Dan Carroll
Dan Cline & The Browns Line
Dan DaRe - Summerville, SC
Dan Hungerman
Dan Kevany
Dan Lalich
Dan Linsalata
Dan Marks
Dan Ott
Dan Rimelspach
Dane Gardner
Daniel Leis
Daniel Levak
Danny Brown
Danny Fonovic
Danny, the Champion of the World
Dar Adams
Darren Rovell
Dave and Charlie Neff
Dave Beals - DaveBealsComedy.com
Dave Kraszewski...dedicated to Uncle Frank
Dave Kundrach
Dave Michael
Dave Peterson
Dave Strasburg
David "Long Suffering" Sekerak
David Alan Kennedy
David Eppler
David Kline
David Lemmeyer
David Ludwig
David N. Vaughn
David Planitz
David V. Spencer

David Weidner
David, Carrie & Conner Phillippi
Dawn Sebock
Debdut Dudebro Biswas
Deborah A. Weber
Deborah Goodere
Delaney Daum
Derek Chan
DERF
Diana Prokopovich
Diana Vanucci
Diane Jost
Dominic Joseph Chill
Don "Wahoo" Hohler
Don Harnett
Don Price
Donald J Zinner
Donald Joseph Kingsbury
Donald Mackay Wonderly
Dooooogan
Double D
Doug & Erynn Rathburn
Doug Dvorak Jr. and the Dvorak family
Doug Root
Doug Thorne
Douglas Steller
Dr. Chris Walker: 2smart2cheer4CLE!
Dr. Kurtis Dornan
Drew Karode
Duane Foy
Dubinsky Family
Duran Yancy
Dylan Ashe
Earnest "Big Earn" Henry
Ed Marszal
Ed Paget
Ed Sweeney
Eddie Stall
Edgar Jones Basketball League
Eli Johnson
Elisa Huenefeld
Elsley Family
Elyce Henkin & Family
Eric Bucher

Eric Dodds
Eric Eilberg & Alysse Boyd
Eric Knappenberger
Eric T. Rapp
Eric Wittine
Erik "Next Year" Flesher
Erik Zumsteg
Erin McGee
Erin Shea Gething
Erotic Pony
Felix Kambouropoulos
FirstandLexington.com
Flacks family Cleveland sports fans
For Greg Toth, lifelong sufferer
Forrest Joseph 'The Drive' Bowlick
Frank Zgrabik
Fred Dillon
Gabe Rhoads
Gary A Seitz
Gary Copeland
Gary Fairchild
Gary, Jeremy and Jason Laughlin
Geoff Gottlieb
Geoffrey Tittyung
Geoffrey Turbow
George and Kathy Mathewson
George J Bokla
Ginger Cringer
gloria mcknight
Go Tigers, Pistons, and... uh... Lions....
GOATNECK
Grandpa Landis
Greg Lawless & Parker Fehrenbach
Greg Sirpilla
Gregory Earls
Griffen Hollow Studio
Griffin Schuele
Haewan & Patrick Green
Haley & Kirsten Erickson
Hallie Beth Albert
Hallie Sheck
Hannah Smith's dad Matt
Happy 60th Birthday Pat Hovance!
Harlan R. Sayles, Esq.

Harry D. Matter
Harvey R. Freeman
Heather Petteys
Heidi Patterson
Here We Go Brownies, Here We Go! PJW
Hiram's Mad Organist
Hoge Hollo
Howard Hill
Iacano Family
Ian M.
Igor Ramone
In honor of Steve Meli & John Shutsa
In memory of Brother Jody Hoop. A
        true Browns fan. - Tim Allen
In memory of Katherine Martin
In memory of my Dad, Ben Skonieczny
Inmate # 1809197-813 Wiemer,Andrew C
Ira & Marcy Young
J. Fred LIndner
J. R. Tracy
J. Robinson
J.B. & Stephanie Harmon
Jack Hay
Jacob Floyd
Jacob Thomas David Radsick
Jacqueline M. Munyasya
Jake Palmer
James DeVoe
James O'Neill
James S. Anderson
Jamie Falcon
Jamie Merz
Jamie Van Pelt (you're welcome, Cindy)
Jane Milauskas
Jason and Lynn Glarner
Jason Beaumont
Jason Craw
Jason Hall
Jason McCarthy
Jason Mulvin
Jason Plautz
Jason R. Glista
Jason Turowski
Jay Edwards

Jay Lyons
Jeff "Brownie" Hohler
Jeff & David Cummings, Toronto
Jeff & Tammi Peters
Jeff Bowen
Jeff Davis, Denver CO
Jeff Jewell
Jeff McCullough
Jeff Rechenbach
Jeff Rembrandt
Jeff Taylor
Jeff Yoders
Jeffrey L. Winland
Jennica Bellanca
Jennifer Green Byerly
Jensen Harris
Jeremy Drollinger
Jeremy McGurr
Jeremy Smith
Jeremy William Guy
Jeremy, Skip, and Terry Ward
Jerry Tinianow, die hard Cleveland
    sports fan
Jesse Klein
Jim Angel
Jim Barbosky
Jim Dyer
Jim Kondrat - Here we go Brownies!
Jim Madigan (Chicago, IL)
Jim Szoke
Jim Tocco
Jim, Kathy, and Alicia Friedman
Joanne O'Brien & Anthony Grande, Jr.
Joe Guttenplan
Joe Javorsky
Joe Table
Joe Tomino
Joe Veto
Joe Wos
Joel "The Weasel" Dorsey
Joel Neckers
Joemoni thing 1&2 Fratena
John & Terri Lynagh
John A Martello

John A. Martin
John and Linda Ceol
John Byrnes
John Clendenning
John Kelley
John Parente
John Sheppard
John Stephen Trapp Jr
John Vinesky, Lowcountry Browns Backer
John W. Secrest
John, Amy, & Annora Jeffries
Jon & Ligia Markman
Jon Brahler
Jon Eisner
Jonathan & Lindsey Schulz
Jonathan Eggleton
Jonathan Hildebrandt
Jonathan Maag
Jonathan Massie
Joseph Forgacs
Joseph M. Biegacki
Joseph Miniaci
Joseph P. Divers
Josephine Steiner
Josh Epstein
Josh Friedman
Joshua Rosen
Joshua S Braun
jouser
Joy Jones Wallace & Family JR
Jubes
Jud Horning & Drew Polen
Judy Appleton
Judy Phillips
Juli (LoGuidice) Kernodle
Julia Aromatorio
Julia Kwong
Julie and Jim Lach
Julie Graf
Justin
Justin Gottshall
Justin Groza
Justin K Rising
Justin Kurzweil

Justin Williams (Cleveland Steamer)
Justin, Jenn, and Reagan Drummond
K. Gregorski
Kaitlin Wallace
Kanak "Brownbear" Chatterjee
Karen
Karen Green
Karen Hill, Canton
Karena Hope Williams
Karl Sanderson
Kate Bradley Fergus
Kathleen Burke, Best Sister-In-Law Ever
Kathryn Lambert and Chris Dillon
Kathy (Brown's FOREVER FAN)
Kathy Cocuzzi
Kathy Lyle
Kathy 'We'll get it THIS year' Hanning
Katie Hutchison & Josh Schnitzler
Katie Voroselo
Keith (Kosar - let's get a drink) Rowe
kelly
Ken & Colleen Mertes
KenBob Watson & Family
Kenneth Danford
Kevin
Kevin "My Dad" & Sue O'Brien
Kevin and Sam Bantner
Kevin J Linden
Kevin Nowland - Go Blue!
Kim House
Kirk Robinson
Kobustabus
Kristy Gallo
Kurt Krol
Kyle Edwards
Kyle Lowry
Landen Sookoo
Larry "Los Gigantes" Norcini
Larry E Harness
Larry Feld
Larry Lev (in memory of Herb)
Larry Luciano
Laura Graven
Lauren Bloomberg

Lauren Brown
Lauren Bruns
Laverne Trzaska Waskielis
Leah C Guinn
Lee Nicholas
LeeAnne Brummer
LeeAnne Sipe
Len Davis
Linda McGrath
Lisa Lucilio
Lisa Manson
Little Joey Kimosh
Lorren Koppelman
Luke Keller
Luke Rizzo
M. Calkins
M. Carson   www.vermontpickle.com
MadMike Beucler
MAhn: [nowinsok: CLE]. Happy Birthday!
Marc Lantos
Marco Ruffini
Maria Caldwell Nosse
Mark Czajkowski
Mark Fischer
Mark Hanson
Mark J Sherman
Mark Moll
Mark Stanley
Mary Hussey (Nicoletti)
Mary Weatherhead Feldman
Matt B & Christian E, diehard fans
Matt Crum
Matt Kalister
Matt Lazar
Matt Markowski
Matt Mitchell
Matt Reno
Matt Ribic
Matt Wells
Matt Yanchar
Matt, Cory, Marty Bretz & Josh Vickers
Matthew "Matty" Johnston
Matthew B. Thomson
Matthew D. Bailey

Matthew Frye
Matthew J. Hawley, Esq,
Matthew Kelner
Matthew Philip Wee
Matthew Sprague
Matthew Watson
Matthew Wright
Max Sirak
Max Yuan
Maybe next year, or the year after... DS
Meghan Lindenberger
Melanie Robinson
Melissa Dale
Meshugga Mayton Wonderly
Michael "Aviator" Fulop
Michael A. Disbrow
Michael Beach
Michael Bokar
Michael Bradley Perry & Family
Michael Chu
Michael Cicchiani
Michael Davis
Michael Frey
Michael G. Baker
Michael Kus
Michael Marshburn
Michael Moyles
Michael S. Ryan
Mike "Butch" Rohan
Mike & Laura Elsigian
Mike and Elizabeth Carruth
Mike Beyersdoerfer
Mike Bresnahan
Mike D.
Mike Donovan
Mike Durst
Mike Ellis - Rocky River via Warren, OH
Mike Guptil - cause Cleveland rocks
Mike Harsh
Mike Jacobs, #1 Cleveland fan, win or lose!
Mike Kertesz
Mike Lonesky
Mike Macksood... WHO DEY !
Mike Menner

Mike Miller
Mike Nardis
Mike Neff
Mike Osenar
Mike Selden
Mike Southmayd
Mike Stagl
Mike Van Dorn
Mike Wasylenky
Mike Wittine
Mike, Ciara & Kierin Querubin
Milton M Fish
Mitch Guttenplan
Monica Kropp - Semper Fi
Mr Steve Marhevka and Dr Ruth
Malenda
Myles A Simmons
N Shah
Nancy Baxter
Nancy Loren
Nate Purinton
Nathan "Pops" Pappalardo
Nathan "Why Am I A Fan Again?" Osborn
Nathan Starr
Nathaniel and Joshua Fronek
Ned The Mailman
Neil & Monica Stelkic
Neil Gogate
Neil, Connie, Drew & Peter Waxman
Nicholas Jump
Nick Panno
Nick Rericha
Nick Schiltz
Nick Sertell & Ella Thompson
Noah Szubski & Bernie Kosar
Noonsongyi and Scott
Nyam Rembert
Orange and Brown Dawg Pound #606
Pam Beil Jimmy Lavin Serenity Hansen
Parry Keller
Parry Tsangaris
Pat Hu (witnessed Jordan's shot over Ehlo
    in person at age 10)
Patrick G. Flynn

Patrick M. Hamlin
Patrick Mechenbier
Patrick Santilli
Patrick Thornton
Paul & Barbara Tyler
Paul Ip & The Yellow Bellies
Paul Spencer
Paul Tagliamonte
Paul Weirtz 64 wait.
Pete & Joan Priola
Peter I. Minton
Phillip G. Ponder, Jr.
Pigskin 'n Pearls
Pittsburgh Steelers and fans
Princess Stephanie Galambos
R. Cortlandt Heroy
Rachel Duleba
Rakesh Kilaru
Ralph Weiser
Randolph N. Townley
Randy & Jason Taylor
Rebecca Hoenigman
Reese and Zoe P's Dad
Rich & Kathi Honig
Rich and Peg Pountney
Richard E. Logan
Rick Drushal
Rob and Karli Mullally
Rob Soccorsi
Robb Szybisty
Robert & Nancy Henry
Robert Allen Nicholson
Robert Baird Murray III
Robert Burns
Robert Darr
Robert Edgecomb & Amie Medley
Robert L. Nicnolson
Robert W Voltz
Roland W. Riggs IV
Ron Kalasunas
Roz & Joanne Gibson
RStrozak #SoCleveland #ClassicKate
Russell Robertson
Ryan & Scotty Deaner

Ryan Beal
ryan coakley
Ryan Haas
Ryan Hrabusa
Ryan Sirpilla
Ryan Travalik
Ryne DiPerna
S. Castlebury
Sam Piatt
Sam Utley
Sam Wager
Samantha Santos
Samuel Lam
Sandra
Sara Enos
Sarah Weber
Scott "Cicada" Crislip
Scott Cannon
Scott Chitwood
Scott Duckworth - Lifetime Fan of
   hopeful sadness
Scott Seidel
Scott Siegel
Scott Williams
Sean McGurr
Sean Michael Bergin
Seth Linnick
Shane Powers
Shane Willoughby
Shanthi Bry
Shawn & Emily Everhart
Shawn Oyler
Shawn W. Beres
Sheilah Villari
Shelley Benson, in memory of Bob Benson
Sheri L Meier
Sherri & Craig Shubert
Sherri Ryder
Sherry and Warren Brown
Sir jason the feinberg
Sky Daniels
Stacy McDade
Steinbrunner Family
Stephanie Liscio

Stephanie M. Boyle
stephen
Stephen Fogg a DieHard Fan and Father
Stephen McClune
Stephen Michael Gyor
Steve and Andy Quinn
Steve Braswell
Steve Kowal
Steve Leonard
Steve Matchinga
Steve Michalec
Steve Neff
Steve Saferin
Steve Spence
Steven Bodie
Steven C. Hatch
Steven Cushner
Steven J. Shrock
Steven McAlonis
Stevie Beshire
Stuart Zaas
Susan B Lang
Susan Rainford
Svarovsky family
Taggart's Pub - Class of 2008
Tara Johnson
Ted Gibson
Ted Wagner
Teresa Folger
Terry Warner
The Ahmads
The Arnson Family
The Boz
The Bryan Hamilton Family
The Burke/Fuerst Family of CLE HTS
The Chuhay & Dombroskas Families
The Danners
The Freemals
The Garvin & Gerstenberger Families
The Gehrisch Family
The General is coming for your knees!
The George Family, Bath Township, OH
The Gollinger Family
The Gray Family of Myersville, MD

The Grincius'
The Guba Family
The Hebrew-Prayers-on-the-Floor Coles
The Hoover Family
The Hora Family
The Howard Family (Don, Angela & Reid)
The Howdyshell's
The Huth Family
The Kearneys
The Kirtz Brothers
The Longsuffering Simons
The Lundeen and McGarry fam
The May Family
THE Mike Jonke
The Paul Family
The Pennock and Ehresman Kids
The Rafal Family
The Ream Family (Pittsburgh sucks!)
The Saunders Family
The Schwab Family
The Scott Daubenmire Family
The Shooks of NM & OH
The Slocums
The Society CFHS '86
The Strah Family
The Tam/Phoenix Family
The Yanchar Family
Theodore George Cherpas
Thomas J. Dirmyer
Thomas Mis
Thomas Nelson Scott
Thomas Winfield Jacobs
Tim "Menzie" Menz
Tim & Jackie Ackerman
Tim Bajorek
Tim Beckner
Tim Markman
TIM RAMSIER
Tim Reza
Tim Schwirtz's Fault
Timmy Goldberg
Timothy O'Kane
Timothy Sekula
TJ and Grant

TK
To Burf: Larry and Beth Cobler
To Dale - Love Mom
Todd & Cody Ceol Charlotte Backers
Todd A Odess
Todd and Troy Stowe
Todd Galloway
Todd Shane Hill
Tom & Diane Fulkerson
Tom Debo
Tom Lowery
Tom Mann
Tom O'Neill
Tom Ritter
Tom Southworth
Tom,Jenni,Josh,Zach,James,Ryan Kuty
Tomek Glinkowski
Tommy Guy Simeone
Trevor "once before I die" Seech

Umbaugh
Valerie Simeone
Vincent Delsanter II
Wade Varner
Wally, David, and Grady Kent
Wandy
Warren G. Hanes
Warren Wilding
Warren, Vivian, Zach and Ryan Rose
Why LeBron Why
Will "BigBadBrowni" Mercer
Will Karim
William Mansour
With Sympathy, Tim Hughes
www.showyourtix.com for Browns tickets
Yancey Strickler
Zach, Amber, and Carter Twarek
Zachary Schellhase
Zack Hansen

Order online:
www.CLEcoloringbook.com

 @CLEsportsBummer    CLEcoloringbook

CPSIA information can be obtained
at www.ICGtesting.com
Printed in the USA
BVOW08s1104030617

485633BV00005B/35/P